The Ugliest

THE NUBIAN VULTURE

THE SOUTHERN ELEPHANT SEAL

THE BABIRUSA

THE NAKED MOLE RAT

THE PROBOSCIS MONKEY

THE CASQUE-HEADED TREE FROG

THE FROGFISH

THE PIPA PIPA TOAD

THE JACKSON'S CHAMELEON

THE OCTOPUS

THE BALD UAKARI

THE PORCUPINE FISH

RANDOM HOUSE 🏠 NEW YORK

Address: Africa and the Arabian Peninsula

Size: A little over 3 feet long

Weight: About 13 pounds

The Nubian Vulture

This scavenger— with its naked head and neck— is a most useful garbage collector....

This cousin of the eagle soars above the savanna like a glider, spreading its wings, which measure over 3 feet long each. The plains are littered with dead or dying animals. Some are old, sick, or injured; some were killed during fights; and others are the leftovers from a carnivore's feast. When the Nubian vulture's sharp eye spots one of these unfortunate creatures, it dives straight for it. The vulture's featherless neck and head are well adapted to carrion consuming. When the giant bird withdraws its neck and head from a carcass, they are covered with blood.

Fortunately, because there are no feathers on the head for the blood to stick to, it dries quickly and flakes off the vulture's head in the hot sun.

The Nubian vulture's powerful beak can break the bones of its prey into a thousand pieces. The vulture swallows muscle, skin, and meat. Only lions and hyenas are able to interrupt its feast. The vulture can eat over 2 pounds of meat at each meal. It is a useful scavenger. By ridding the environment of rotting flesh, it keeps colonies of germ-carrying flies in check.

The Southern Elephant Seal

The enormous, 4-ton male seal can inflate his nose till it doubles in size!

Heave ho! In September, male elephant seals heave themselves—burdened under thick layers of fat, and with much groaning—out of the water and onto the sandy beach. It's almost mating season, and everyone wants the best spots for attracting the ladies.

To intimidate each other, the elephant seal males blast threatening sounds from their big gray noses—noses that measure over 15 inches long! Their groans are anything but melodious. The huge, lumpy animals lunge at each other, bellowing all the while. Holding themselves almost erect, they measure twice the average height of a person!

Battles between these gigantic sea mammals can last half an hour and often leave both rivals wounded. The winners become the leaders of the elephant seal colony.

But during mating season, they have only one thing in mind: charming a harem of chubby young females!

The fatter the elephant seal, the more attractive it is. That's why before mating season begins, the male and female elephant seals make a special effort to pack on the pounds. They dive over 3,800 feet deep in the water, where they gorge themselves on squid and fish without any competition. After feeding like this for up to 2 hours, they return happily to the surface.

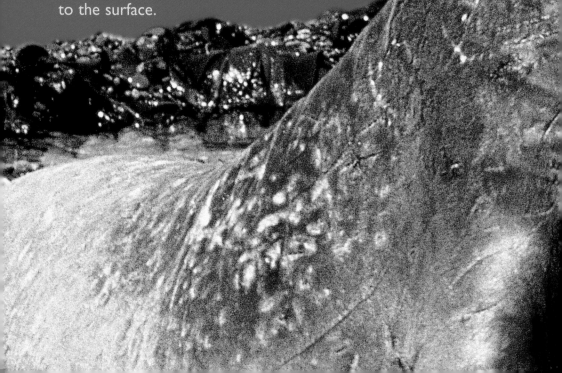

Address: South Georgia Island, the Falkland Islands, and Patagonia, Argentina

Size: Male: Up to 20 feet long
Female: Up to 10 feet long

Weight: Male: From 6,600 to 8,000 pounds
Female: Up to 1,300 pounds

Favorite food: Squid and fish

Patagonia,
Argentina
South Georgia Island
Falkland Islands

Indonesia

Address: Indonesia
Size: About 3.5 feet long
Weight: Up to 220 pounds
Favorite food: Leaves, shoots, and fallen fruit

The male babirusa has 4 tusks: 2 that are sharply curved and 2 that are less curved. The most amazing of these tusks are the 2 that grow through the top of the male's muzzle. The older a male babirusa gets, the longer these grow. In curving backward, these gigantic teeth can reach the babirusa's forehead. Sometimes they even grow back into the animal's head!

The female babirusa has canines that are much smaller.

In the wild, babirusas can easily crack hard nuts with their rigid teeth. They feed mainly on leaves, shoots, and fruits. They do not root in the ground like other species of pigs, but do on occasion use their teeth to dig insects out of rotting trees.

To defend itself, the babirusa brandishes its tusks as if they were swords. The curved upper canines are not well suited for injuring opponents, but are quite useful in warding off attack!

An excellent swimmer, the babirusa uses its 200-pound body like a buoy and can float from island to island to feast on fruit.

The babirusa is a shy animal and runs from the presence of humans—and who can blame it? The creature has been widely hunted for its meat. Today, the species is endangered.

The Bab

The babirusa has 2 giant canines that protrude through its upper jaw—and can even puncture its own skull!

irusa

Africa

Address: Kenya, Somalia, and Ethiopia

Size: From 3 to 4 inches long, plus a 1-to-2-inch-long tail

Weight: From .75 to 2.8 ounces

Favorite food: Worms, insect larvae, tubers, and roots

This charming rodent obeys a queen, who reigns over an immense underground gallery. . . .

The naked mole rat is deaf, blind, and nearly bald. It moves about under the ground using a mustache of whiskers, called "vibrissae," to guide itself. Unlike other mammals, the naked mole rat has almost no ability to regulate its body temperature. Its nearly hairless skin allows it to absorb heat more quickly.

Mole rats form colonies that contain up to 300 individuals and are the largest cooperative breeding groups known among mammals. They serve a queen (who is just as ugly as her subjects!). She is the longest rodent in the colony.

Their long teeth are extremely strong. The mole rats use them to dig through ground as hard as concrete and make tunnels as long as several football fields!

Some mole rats are assigned the job of guarding the gallery. Others take care of the young or are in charge of finding food. They use their teeth to dig up roots and tubers that are rich in water and sugar. Some enterprising mole rats actually "farm" food: they eat only part of a tuber, allowing it to continue to grow . . . and to supply more food!

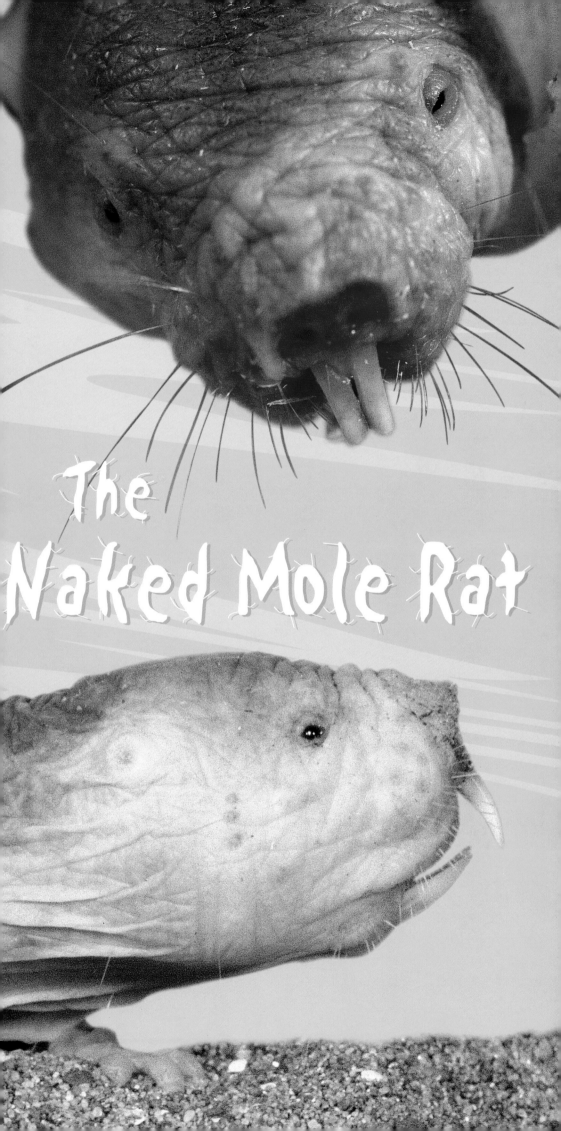

The Naked Mole Rat

The strange-looking male proboscis monkey, with his cucumber-like nose, lives with a group of about 10 females. The ladies—who have pointy little, upturned snouts—select a male together, and his nose must be at least 3 inches long. That's because at this length, the proud proboscis monkey starts to "talk" from his nose. The monstrous appendage actually helps amplify the male's voice. And he can stand the nose up high to make it honk even better!

When he's in a bad mood, the proboscis monkey puffs up his nose as it reddens with anger.

Both male and female proboscis monkeys are born with tiny, upturned noses. They are cared for by nannies, who are assisted by the strangest granddaddy. His nose has grown so long, it hangs beneath his chin like a tie! Gramps has to push it aside with his hands to get food into his mouth!

THE PROBOSCIS MONKEY

The longer the nose, the better-looking the monkey!

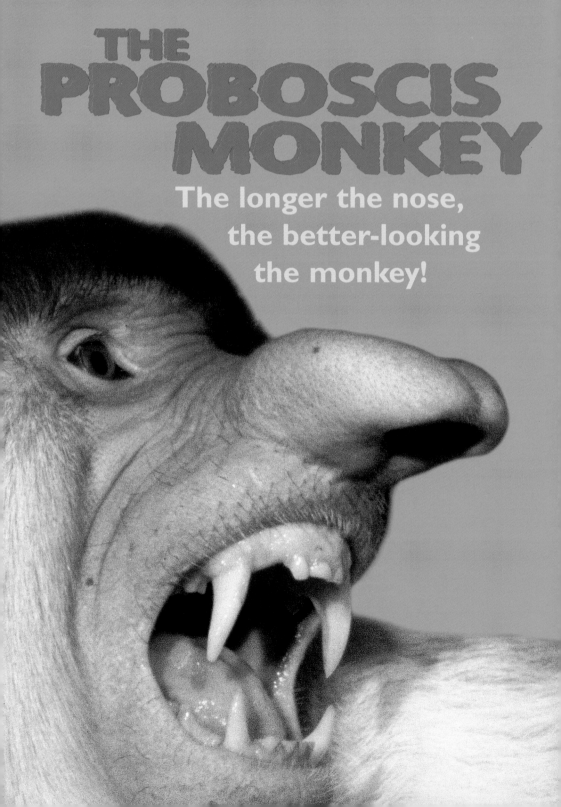

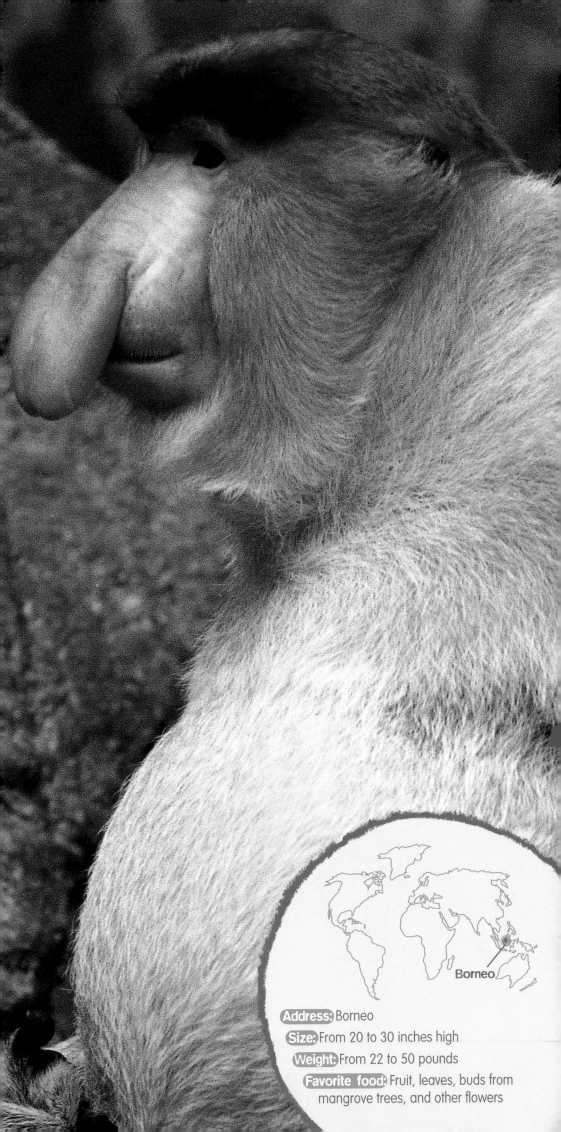

Address: Borneo

Size: From 20 to 30 inches high

Weight: From 22 to 50 pounds

Favorite food: Fruit, leaves, buds from mangrove trees, and other flowers

The Casque-Headed Tree Frog

By perching in the branches of trees, this Mexican frog is able to avoid many predators in the tropical forest. But if one should approach, this clever little frog has a plan: it backs up *inside* the tree's trunk! Tucked under the bark, the tree frog will stay there motionless, using its "helmet" to block the entrance to its hiding spot!

During the rainy season, the casque-headed tree frog likes to take showers in the rain. The water soaks into its skin, which is thin and porous.

By nightfall, the casque-headed tree frog is ready for a good meal. When evening comes, it sticks its long snout out of the tree trunk to feast on hundreds of insects.

The casque-headed tree frog is a real acrobat—but there's little risk of its falling from the branches. The tips of its toes provide traction, like nonslip soles!

With its head cloaked in a helmet, this tree frog is dressed like a toy soldier!

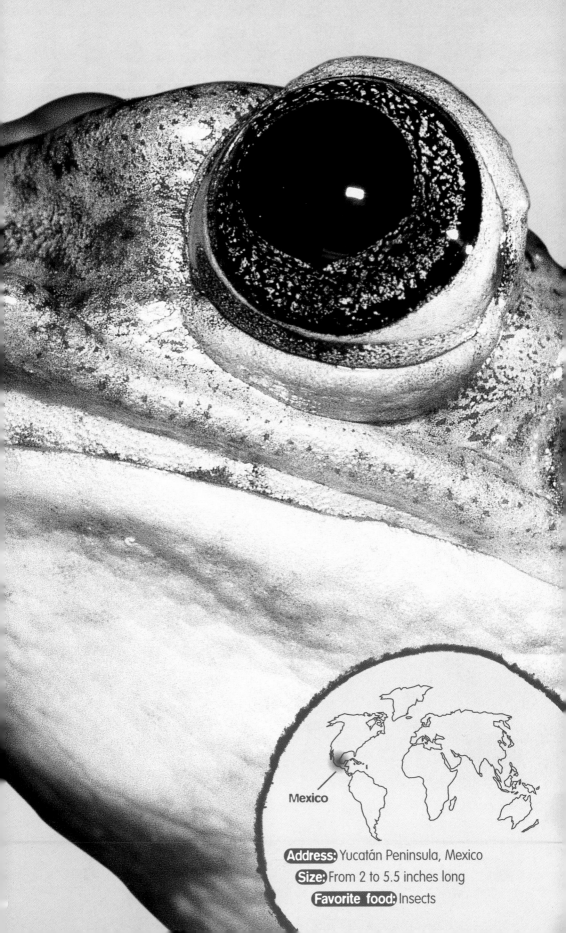

Mexico

Address: Yucatán Peninsula, Mexico
Size: From 2 to 5.5 inches long
Favorite food: Insects

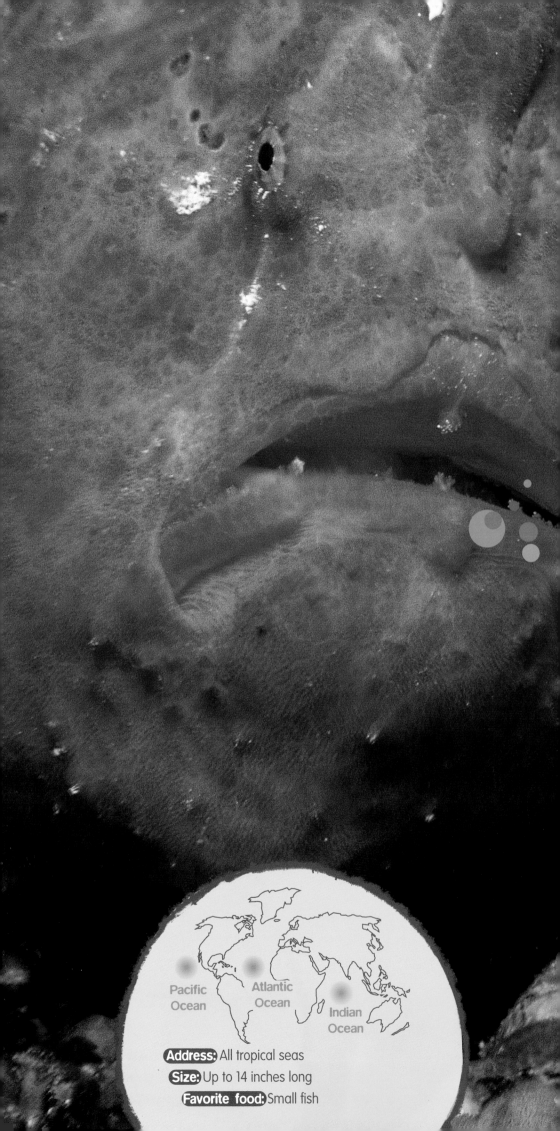

Address: All tropical seas

Size: Up to 14 inches long

Favorite food: Small fish

Now you see it, now you don't! This fish looks so much like a rock, it seems part of the reef. . . .

The Frogfish

Its skin is neither beautiful nor smooth. It's as rough as a block of stone. The frogfish takes on the same colors as its underwater hiding places, where it lives as deep as 165 feet below the surface! Some species are reddish brown, like coral reefs; others are light brown, like the sandy sea bottom.

The frogfish belongs to the anglerfish family. The first dorsal spine on its head looks like a wire with a piece of bait dangling from its end. The frogfish uses this odd physical attribute like a fishing pole! By wiggling itself, the frogfish jiggles the "bait," attracting smaller fish. Then it opens its jaws wide and gulps down the confused prey.

Sometimes, the frogfish stops swimming and "stands up" on the fins on its belly. It uses these pectoral fins, shaped like palmed feet, as, well . . . feet, and actually seems to walk underwater!

There are some 40 species of frogfish. Some are no bigger than an oyster. Others are the size of a football—and swallow fish as big as themselves!

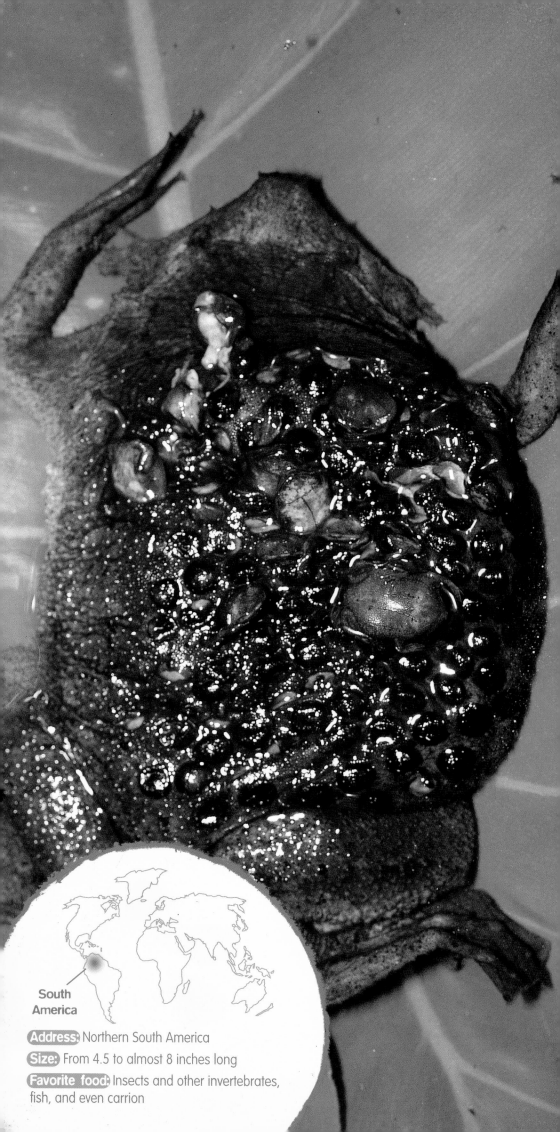

South America

Address: Northern South America

Size: From 4.5 to almost 8 inches long

Favorite food: Insects and other invertebrates, fish, and even carrion

The Pipa Pipa Toad

Pass the acne medicine! The female of this species is so ugly, she looks as if she's covered with pimples. . . .

Pipa pipa toads are fat and have flat bodies that look as if they've been run over by a truck. Their skin is the color of dead leaves. This stylish outfit enables them to camouflage themselves in the swampy waters of Guiana and the Amazon.

It's during the mating season that the female pipa pipa toad becomes especially ugly. Fortunately, there's good reason for this. After the female lays her 50 to 100 eggs, they sink *into* her skin! Her back thickens and she starts to look like a thin inflatable mattress. By doing this, the female protects each of her eggs in a tiny nest of skin, where it can grow in a safe environment. During this period, the female's bumpy back looks as if it is covered with pimples. After 2 months, each baby leaves its little "house" by piercing the hood of skin protecting it!

Unlike other frogs and toads, baby pipa pipa toads do not hatch as tadpoles but are fully formed toadlets from the beginning.

These toads are great carnivores. With their big mouths, they eat anything that they can shove in with their front legs. Fish, insects, and even other frogs: nothing that fits in their mouths is safe!

Africa

Address: East Africa

Size: About 4.5 inches long, plus a 7-inch-long tail

Weight: From 1.75 to 3 ounces

Favorite food: Insects and spiders

Wearing its headdress of 3 horns, the male looks like a miniature Triceratops!

Despite its funny looks, the Jackson's chameleon is serious about catching insects. With one eye, the chameleon can observe the prey in front of it—and with the other eye, it can watch the area behind it! Thanks to these independently moving eyes—and a tail that can be used for grasping—the Jackson's chameleon can stay motionless on a tree branch for hours, waiting for its next victim.

Then in a split second, the hungry lizard's tongue shoots out of its mouth. Covered in sticky saliva, it captures an insect (which cannot get unstuck!). After swallowing its prey, the lizard retracts its long tongue back inside its mouth.

The Jackson's chameleon's skin color can change according to its emotions and surroundings. It has no trouble camouflaging itself out-of-doors.

The female Jackson's chameleon doesn't have any horns. But at birth, her male babies have tiny mini-horns!

The Jackson's Chameleon

Without its arms—which look as if they're covered with warts—the octopus couldn't move. It uses them to swim, to hold on to rocks, and to grab its food.

At nightfall or at dawn, the octopus comes out of its underwater shelter to search for food. Mollusks and shellfish taken prisoner under its hundreds of suction cups are helpless to make an escape.

Some octopuses are able to inject venomous saliva into their prey. Because the octopus's mouth resembles a parrot's beak, all it has to do is crack the shells of crabs and lobsters and suck in their delicious meat!

To defend itself against enemies (such as the moray eel), the octopus ejects a thick stream of black ink. While its attackers are blinded by this horrible cloud, the octopus can beat a hasty retreat.

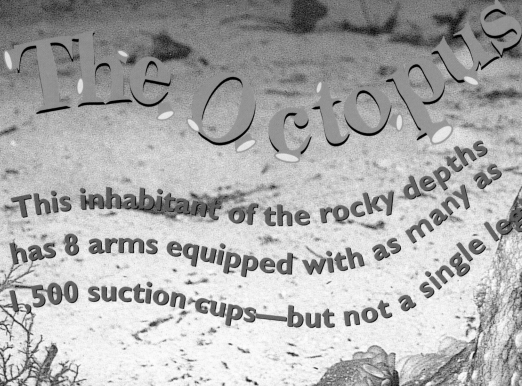

The Octopus

This inhabitant of the rocky depths has 8 arms equipped with as many as 1,500 suction cups—but not a single leg!

English Channel

Mediterranean Sea

Atlantic Ocean

Pacific Ocean

Address: The Pacific Ocean, the Atlantic Ocean, the English Channel, and the Mediterranean Sea

Size: From 1 inch to over 16 feet wide

Weight: Up to 90 pounds

Favorite food: Crabs, lobsters, and shellfish

To camouflage itself, the octopus has another trick: like the chameleon, it changes color depending on its location. Its skin can appear full of holes and bumps, just like the rocks in which it hides!

The female octopus is an attentive mother. She lays from 200,000 to 400,000 eggs, each as tiny as a grain of rice. After she lays them, she stops eating so as not to leave them alone for a single second.

After the eggs hatch, the mother octopus dies of exhaustion—and hunger. Talk about dedication!

South America

Address: The Amazon River in Brazil and Peru, and Colombia

Size: About 21 inches long, plus a 6-inch-long tail

Weight: About 7 pounds

Favorite food: Seeds, fruit, and flowers

The Bald Uakari

This monkey's face is so red, it always looks mad....

But there's little chance of a bald uakari getting angry—they're peaceful monkeys!

When its face deepens from pink to poppy red, that means it's frightened. And in the tropical forest, this monkey has plenty to frighten it.

When facing a harpy eagle—a bird of prey capable of capturing a monkey with a single swipe of its claws—the uakari just can't compete. Under its thick coat of fur (which reveals only its hands and bald head), this monkey is no bigger than a cat!

The uakari rarely leaves the treetops. On the ground, a jaguar would need only one gulp to devour it. Is it any wonder, then, that even when it's young, the uakari looks old?

The uakari is no safer taking a cool dip. The swampy waters where it lives are infested with small predator fish, like the voracious piranha—and big snakes, like the anaconda!

There's strength in numbers. In groups, uakari monkeys are less fearful. That's why they live in troops of 10 to 50 monkeys. To find each other among the leafy branches, they screech—and appear to make faces at each other!

Surrounded by thick clouds of mosquitoes, they munch on fruit to quench their thirst.

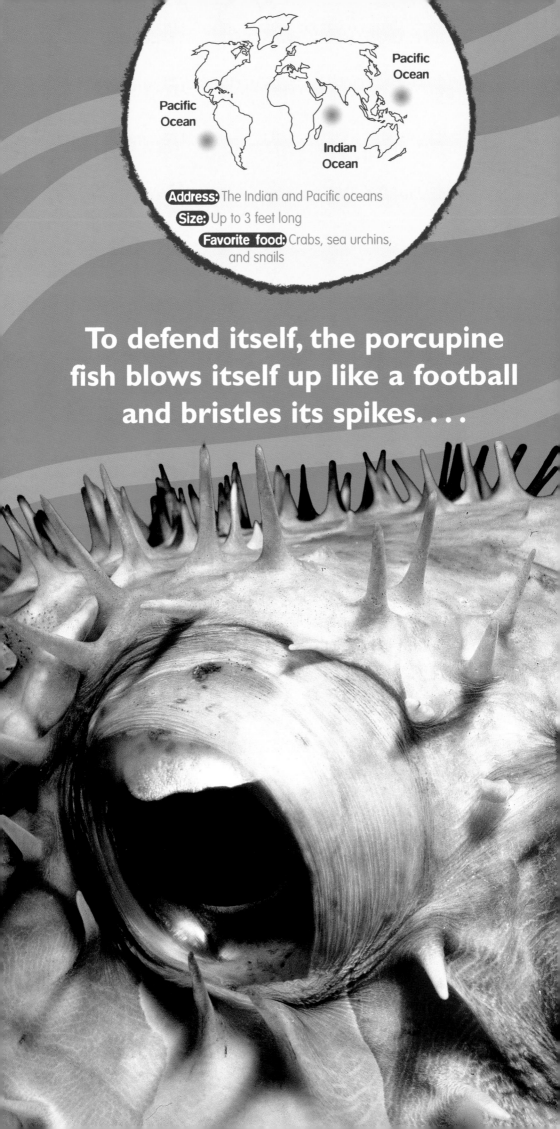

Pacific
Ocean

Pacific
Ocean

Indian
Ocean

Address: The Indian and Pacific oceans
Size: Up to 3 feet long
Favorite food: Crabs, sea urchins, and snails

To defend itself, the porcupine fish blows itself up like a football and bristles its spikes. . . .

The Porcupine Fish

When at rest, this inhabitant of the tropical seas looks entirely harmless. It's long and oval, with thick spikes folded against its body. Swimming quietly among the coral reefs, it hides its true self very well.

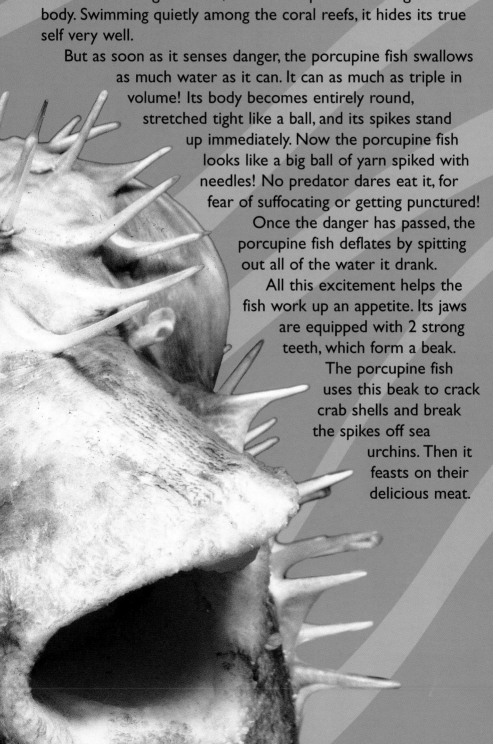

But as soon as it senses danger, the porcupine fish swallows as much water as it can. It can as much as triple in volume! Its body becomes entirely round, stretched tight like a ball, and its spikes stand up immediately. Now the porcupine fish looks like a big ball of yarn spiked with needles! No predator dares eat it, for fear of suffocating or getting punctured! Once the danger has passed, the porcupine fish deflates by spitting out all of the water it drank.

All this excitement helps the fish work up an appetite. Its jaws are equipped with 2 strong teeth, which form a beak. The porcupine fish uses this beak to crack crab shells and break the spikes off sea urchins. Then it feasts on their delicious meat.

The Funny-Face Club

THE SOUTHERN ELEPHANT SEAL

THE CASQUE-HEADED TREE FROG

THE PIPA PIPA TOAD

THE NUBIAN VULTURE

THE PROBOSCIS MONKEY

THE NAKED MOLE RAT

THE FROGFISH

THE OCTOPUS

THE BALD UAKARI

THE JACKSON'S CHAMELEON

THE BABIRUSA

THE PORCUPINE FISH

Know someone
who should
join this club?
Paste his or her
picture here!

Know someone
who should
join this club?
Paste his or her
picture here!

Photographs:
Bald uakari: left, D. Heuclin/BIOS; right, Seitre/BIOS.
Nubian vulture: left, X. Eichaker/BIOS; right, L. Renaud/BIOS.
Octopus: F. Bavendam/BIOS.
Jackson's chameleon: left, M. Harvey/BIOS; right, D. Heuclin/BIOS.
Naked mole rat: middle, A. Odum/Peter Arnold/BIOS; right, Seitre/BIOS.
Pipa pipa toad: D. Heuclin/BIOS. Babirusa: A. Compost/BIOS.
Frogfish: Y. Lefevre/BIOS.
Proboscis monkey: left, Bildarchiv/OKAPIA/BIOS; cover and right interior,
P. Weimann/BIOS.
Porcupine fish: left, J. Rotman/BIOS; right, J. Rotman/Peter Arnold/BIOS.
Southern elephant seal: A. Visage/PHO.N.E.
Casque-headed tree frog: J. Cancalosi/Peter Arnold/BIOS.

First American edition, 2002

Library of Congress Cataloging-in-Publication Data
Doinet, Mymi. The ugliest / [Mymi Doinet].
   p.   cm. — (Faces of nature)
ISBN 0-375-81409-4
1. Animals—Juvenile literature. 2. Morphology (Animals)—Juvenile literature.
[1. Morphology (Animals). 2. Adaptation (Biology). 3. Animals.]
1. Title.   QL49 .D63 2002   590—dc21   2001019277

www.randomhouse.com/kids

Printed in Malaysia February 2002   10 9 8 7 6 5 4 3 2 1
RANDOM HOUSE and colophon are registered trademarks of Random House, Inc.